SECRETS OF THE MUSIC BUSINESS

HOW NOT TO GET FUCKED AS AN ENTREPRENEUR WITH A DREAM

BY
TONY M. FOUNTAIN

Copyright © 2021 by Tony M Fountain
All rights reserved.
For information, visit tonymfountain.com

Library of Congress Control Number: 2021903075
ISBN: 978-1-7366959-0-6
ISBN: 978-1-7366959-1-3 (ebook)

To my precious Cathy and our growing family:
Ian, Tyonna, Hadley, Lexy, and baby Fountain due Summer 2021.

My grandmother Helen Fountain

And for every dreamer,
keep going!

TABLE OF CONTENTS

INTRO 1
THE DECEPTION 3
THE BASICS 7
HOW WEBSITES WORK 15
HOW TO GET PRESS 19
GETTING VERIFIED 26
WATCH YOUR ASS.. 32
KNOW YOUR AUDIENCE.. 36
THE BOTTOM LINE 38
ABOUT THE AUTHOR 41

INTRO

Most artists don't enjoy learning the things they need to succeed with their music. Artists love to create, and taking their attention away from the art itself to focus on other things can be draining, causing the artist to be less creative. There are plenty of children in our public school system that are labeled as rebellious or failing academically. When the real problem is that in laymen's terms, they don't give a fuck about the basic bullshit and would rather be in an art school or at least have more artistic-type classes in their school.

In my humble opinion, students would pay closer attention in school if they were applying their focus to the academia they were interested in.

Unfortunately, for some reason, the government seems only to want to mold everyday workers' minds and not nurture the true passions of our youth.

With that said, I wrote this book to give the artist starting on their journey a quick overview of the things I'm questioned about the most. You will need to do more studying if you really want to learn this game, but this book will cut through a lot of the noise and get you off the porch and running.

THE DECEPTION

The truth is the majority of what you see online is bullshit; smoke and mirrors at its finest! Selling anything from toy cars, music, fast food, or houses is all about how the consumer perceives the product—ever seen a perfect sixty-second trailer for a movie that seems impressive but fails to deliver? Better yet, think about all the people in line for the new game systems or cell phones each year at Christmas when the products hardly have any worthwhile updates, especially for the insane prices they charge. Any gamer with a little bit of a tech background knows you can build a better gaming computer for less than you'd buy a prebuilt one online or in the store.

HYPE Magazine (How You Perceive Everything), in my opinion, has one of the best acronyms around in the entertainment world. It's all about hype when it comes to products and services these days. I mean, come on, they made millions on a shit emoji, for God's sake. Toy Story helped sell a freaking toy fork for $20. I was amazed to see a kid open one while I was at a shop getting new tires. I couldn't believe my eyes; his parents really paid that much for something they could have created themselves at home for $2.

Though we'd like to think that a good song speaks for itself, I disagree entirely, in the short term at least. Unless you're fortunate and randomly go viral, then you could be the next Michael Jackson, and it wouldn't matter. If you don't have a marketing budget to push your project to the masses, the odds of your music organically being discovered are similar to the odds of winning the lottery.

On the other hand, if you've got the money to fund your project, you could be a rainbow-haired rat or a grown-ass man that wears a diaper and go platinum. It's now all about the money and gimmicks in fame and quick jumps in growth. Sadly over half of the songs we receive for review are about cash and riddled with lies. Artists who think they have to create similar content to what's on the radio to make it. Clowns in the circus begging for your attention because, like with sex, attention sells. Attention is why websites have clickbait headlines and why apps like Facebook and Instagram show you more of what the algorithm thinks you're into so they can hold your attention and keep you on the apps longer and make more money from ads etc.

The majority of artists you think are doing fairly well for themselves are barely making minimum wage if anything. You look at their social media engagement, verifications, press coverage, among other things and may think they're wealthy. The truth is they may have an established name but are broke and famous like Rittz says in his song. It takes a lot of time and financial investment to begin seeing an ROI (Return on investment). Sometimes it can be years before an artis ever really sees any money.

A good bit of the time it's prop money, rented cars, friends and relatives homes, and either knock off clothing or apparel from local designers in exchange for the artist wearing the outfits in their posts or performances etc. Though some artist come out and speak on how fake the industry can be, for some reason people still continue to believe otherwise. Don't get me wrong there is money to be made but it's in the long game. If your plans are to get in hit a quick lick and be good to go then you're sadly mistaken.

Once you learn marketing and psychology you'll begin to understand what some refer to as mind control. There are colors, words, and ways to go about posting that can invoke an emotional response from your audience. It's similar to what some people do in dating to form an everlasting attachment by bringing their partner up to an emotional high then it comes crashing back down and then right back up again. Somehow it forms an emotional bond and unfortunately it's why so many stay in abusive relationships. Either way, when using these methods in marketing you can create a loyal fanbase but it's tricks some might even say it's like a form of sorcery.

It does not mean you cannot establish a career in music if you're not willing to play the "game" by any means. Ever heard the saying content is king? It's true if you're going to make a living with music these days, you have to stand above the crowd, and to do that, either you're going to have to create content in various formats constantly, or you're going to have to have a large budget to spread your content. Still, even then, you will need to create consistently.

Once you're verified you will notice that you will be added to engagement groups.

These groups help keep your content at the top and on trending pages. Even before being added to these verified engagement groups you and your friends can still trick the algorithm if you create engagement groups of your own. The way it works is whenever you make a new post you must send the post to the group and everyone in the group has to like and comment on the post immediately and when they make a new post you do the same. The comments have to be authentic and not generic copy and paste or emojis etc. The social platform's algorithm will then will perceive your post to be popular and begin to show it to more people in which case if it is a good post then more organic likes and comments will start coming in and boost your content to the for you page.

THE BASICS

In this chapter, I will attempt to break down some of the basics and discuss how to position yourself to win. We will talk about key terms, rights organizations, LLC vs. Inc, trademarks, and more. This is not to be taken as legal counsel, and I highly recommend further studies.

I'm going to start with some of the words used in the industry. I wish I would have had some of these words broken down for me when I began my journey. Reading and not having everything seem like Greek would have made it a lot easier, so I feel that this is very important for me to go over. I also find that new artists I talk with nowadays struggle in the same way, and most will not even ask what a word means because of pride. Instead, they'll just go along with the conversation and not understand a damn thing you're talking about, which wastes both parties' time. Let me make this clear right out the gate; there's nothing wrong with asking questions if you don't understand something! You better ask as many questions as you need to get a complete understanding of things; otherwise, you're going to fuck yourself in the long run.

Like most artists, I was lost when I first began learning how the music business worked; the acronyms and language used were foreign to me and one of the most complex parts to overcome. It was almost like the authors forgot who their audience was and expected the reader to know the terminology already. This was very frustrating, to say the least, so below, I've chosen a few key sayings that I feel you should know. I won't go too far in-depth, so you will need to do further studying. I've been asked to explain some of these on numerous occasions, so I'll give a brief overview to help you understand a bit before we move forward.

Monetize – When someone speaks about monetization, what they're talking about is a means of making money from your creation. For example, if you record a song today and upload it to Facebook this evening, it wouldn't be monetized because you're not getting paid for it when people listen to the music. You have nothing in place to track the streams, so essentially, you're giving it away free. On the other hand, if you record the song and register it with a PRO, Songtrust, and SoundExchange, then provide it to Facebook via a distributor (DSP) such as Distrokid, it'll be monetized, and the streams and downloads are tracked. Once monetized, you'll be paid royalties for your streams and downloads. There are numerous ways to monetize your music, website, and social media accounts.

Royalties – When someone speaks about royalties in the music business, they are likely referring to the payments due on the backend to all parties involved in creating a song. There are different types of royalties, such as sync, performance, and mechanical.

PRO – Performance rights organization. In the USA, these are BMI, ASCAP, and SESAC. PRO's collect royalties generated by public performance such as radio, clubs, and restaurants.

DSP – Digital service provider. Also known as distributors. DSP's provide your music & videos to iTunes, Spotify, Amazon, and other streaming platforms.

SMM – This stands for social media marketing. In a nutshell, marketing can be various things a company or individual participates in to promote their product. There are different marketing types such as email marketing (email blasts to DJs and blogs) offline marketing, such as posting flyers and handing out CDs. Then, SMM might include influencers to post your content in their Instagram story or have your song reviewed by or product unboxed and compared by famous YouTubers.

PR – PR stands for public relations. These agents take care of you when it comes to press coverage. They help create your story and drive the narrative. They also act as the cleanup crew when there is false information about you spreading like wildfire. Nowadays, a ton of entrepreneurs are playing the PR game. They aren't like the traditional PR agents that create press writeups and pitch your story to news sites to gain you natural coverage by real journalists. A good bit of them are scamming the hell out of people by charging them insane prices or offering guaranteed placements on low-quality websites.

Search engine – It's also referred to as a web browser, which includes but is not limited to Google, Bing, and DuckDuckGo.

RSS – You can think of RSS as a radio or satellite signal. Basically, it's a web code that can be used to automatically transfer your content from one platform to another. For example, you can use RSS to automatically deliver & post your podcast from SoundCloud to iTunes.

For more in-depth reading on the above subjects and more, I suggest picking up the following books.

All you need to know about the music business by Donald S. Passman is first on my list because it pretty much covers everything you need to know, as the title says. It covers topics about your rights, team member roles, how to make money, and much more—written by a lawyer specializing in the music business. If you aren't much of a reader but want to pick up at least one book that will give you the most comprehensive view of the industry, then this is the book for you.

How to make it in the new music business by Ari Herstand is number two on my list because it is from the point of view of a pop artist, so it's slightly different than the first book on my list. Even if you're a hip-hop artist or in a rock band, this book can still be applicable in some aspects and beneficial for you to read.

"How to get a record deal" by Wendy Day comes in third on my list. Written by an industry vet that truly is all about helping artists get what they deserve. Time and again, she has kept artists out of bad deals and assisted in securing good ones. She's worked with artists & labels such as Cash Money Records, MGK, David Banner, Young Jeezy, and more. It's nice to have a book written by someone who indeed does have the artist's best interests at heart.

Now that we've got that out the way let's talk about setting yourself up to win. First and foremost, as an artist, you need to sign up at a few different places to collect your music royalties.

SESAC is an invite-only PRO, so you'll need to choose between ASCAP & BMI. ASCAP charges a small fee of $50 to sign up, and BMI is free. They pretty much offer the same services. I've seen that some artists state they're signed to multiple, but you can only sign with one at a time. Next, you will need to sign up with Sound Exchange. Please note you will need a bank account to sign up with these services to get paid.

You then can set up your own vanity publishing company under a fictitious business name or sign up with Songtrust. Distributors such as CDbaby offer a pro version of their publishing services that includes Songtrust in the bundle.

So now, let's say you've signed up with BMI, Sound Exchange, and Songtrust; what's next? If you're fully dedicated to making this your career, you probably want to apply to get your trademark next. The trademark process can be very lengthy, and if not researched and filed correctly, you may waste your time and money because it's non-refundable. The trademark application will get rejected if it's too similar to one already in use. Trust me, I know because I had to abandon my first attempt at claiming my trademark, so don't go the cheap route. Legal zoom offers to have an attorney take the lead on this process for $600 plus the cost of the filing fees, which vary depending on where you live but average at around $250, give or take.

Something a few don't know about this process is that you should file for your company/artist logo and the name/word as well, which is a separate fee. Also, there is an additional fee for each category you want your trademark to cover. So if you're going to protect your music, clothes, website, etc., with your trademark, these are all separate categories and fees that have to be filed. This can become very expensive, so make damn sure you fully understand what you're getting into before starting this process. But don't wait too long either because someone else may come along and take it before you.

LLC vs. Inc, which is the route to go?

There are a few differences between the two, but for the most part, if you don't plan to make your company publicly tradeable on the stock market, then you don't need an inc. If at a later date you do decide you want to, you can always change it, but for now, your best bet is an LLC. A couple of reasons you want to file for an LLC are to separate your personal assets from your business and for tax purposes. If you get sued for some reason and lose they can only get money from your business and not your personal bank account, home, etc. An LLC protects you and your family hence Limited Liability Company. Filing for a LLC also varies depending on where you live, but again averages at around $250, give or take.

Afterward, you can apply for an EIN (employee identification number) on irs.gov; this part of the process is free. An EIN is like a Social Security number for your business. Now you'll be able to start a business bank account and keep all your personal and business transactions separate. Something else to note is that this will also be something you need later when applying for social media verification. You don't have to, it all depends on how you want to structure your business, but some form multiple LLC's to separate each part of their business. An example of what I mean is you can set up one for your merch and another for touring. You could also set up just one LLC and then file separate DBA's (doing business as), also known in some places as a fictitious business name or trade name.

Next on the list is to start a business Paypal account. Do not confuse a personal PayPal account with the business version. I highly recommend using this payment method afterward for all online transactions because they are the only service that offers protection and give refunds if you don't receive what you paid for. Some international transactions may require Payoneer or Transferwise, so you might as well go ahead and start those while you're at it. Now that you've taken care of the basics, below is a list of other things to look into in the future.

Business STI (state tax ID)

Harry fox agency

ISRC

ISWC

LCCN

Duns & Bradstreet

SIC #

IPI # also referred to as a CAE in the past

Marc21

ISMN

BNF ID

Musicbrains.org

Allmusic.com

Discogs.com

You then need to create a few separate spreadsheets using Microsoft Excel. You need one for all your logins and passwords and another to list information about your releases. The information included should include each song's title, the producer and their contact info, release date, distributor, copyright information, guest appearances and phone number, email, publisher, label, royalty splits, etc. Pretty much everything that someone might need down the line if you happen to run into an issue and maybe need it for court, sign a new distribution or publishing deal, etc.

You don't want to have to spend hours searching for the information. It sucks, I know, but you're in business and have to treat it as such.

You should learn to advertise by taking the Facebook blueprint and Twitter Flight school classes. You also need to be on all platforms even if you don't really care for the app you must be where the consumer can find you. Nowadays people are finding new music on platforms like Tiktok, Triller, and Snapchat. Then if they like the snippet they'll look you up on Spotify, SoundCloud, Audiomack, or iTunes to hear the full song. They then head over to YouTube to check out the video and if they become a fan they'll follow on Facebook, Instagram and others. Once they're super fans they'll want to know more about you, what you stand for, and your thoughts so they'll check you out on Twitter, blogs, and podcasts.

If you don't want things about you known and you would rather live a simple life and not share your experiences with the world then this business isn't for you. Because in this game the people have to feel like they can relate to you and your lifestyle. If you're not genuine and come off fake they will see through it. Ever heard the saying, "give the people what they want?" Well, it's true you have to be transparent.

HOW WEBSITES WORK

There are a ton of websites popping up and disappearing all the time. For the untrained eye, it can be tough to decipher what sites are worthy of your time and which ones aren't. There are people out there in the digital space that create a mass amount of mom-and-pop type sites that may appear visually impressive, but underneath the shiny vail lies great deceit. They have packages of $250 for posts on 150 sites etc. These types of "deals" are of absolutely no value to artists whatsoever, but the allure of having their content posted on so many places for a relatively small price can be quite tempting. These "marketers," aka slithering snakes like that of the serpent in the garden of Eden, know this and come along whispering sweet nothings in their unknowing victims' ears then bite down on their necks like a fledgling vampire tasting his first drop of blood.

You can use tools to learn various things about the websites, such as how many monthly estimated visitors they receive, how authoritative they really are, how long they've been in business, and much more. A few to mention are SimilarWeb, Ahrefs, and MOZ.

Key factors to take a look at when examining a site.

Unlike most things, a lower Alexa score is actually better than a higher Alexa score. Sites that have a lower Alexa are more popular; they receive more traffic and engagement. Generally, a ranking of one million or lower is good.

Domain rating, commonly referred to as (DR), is basically an overall score based on how many and the quality of backlinks a site has.

Backlinks come from various sites linking back to the website you're examining. In a nutshell, they are referral links to said website. They will be DO FOLLOW or NO FOLLOW hyperlinks. DO Follow means that when the bot (known as a spider because it crawls sites) periodically searches websites for new content to index within search results, it will leave the site it's crawling to go to the linked site.

This probably sounds hella confusing, so let me give an example. Suppose I write an article about Yelawolf, and within the second paragraph, I mention Caskey and hyperlink to Caskey's Instagram account with a DO Follow backlink. In that case, the rest of my article about Yelawolf will not be crawled by the spider, and it will not be indexed in google search results. However, if I use a NO Follow backlink to Caskey's Instagram, the bot will note the link but continue reading and indexing the rest of the article on Yelawolf.

Because Do-Follow links lead the bot off the page, typically NO Follow links are used, or if a DO Follow link is used, it's usually placed at the bottom of the article so that the bot indexes everything from that article before leaving the site it's crawling.

For an example of a contextual hyperlink, let's say I write up an article about Bone Thugs -N- Harmony on my site Now Entertainment (site A). Let's pretend I title that article "Fast spitting Midwest rappers," and then afterward, I write another story on Forbes (site B) about the five most influential hip-hop acts of all time. Within the list on Forbes, I could list Bone as one of those acts. To make a good contextual backlink, it has to flow naturally within the article and match the original article's title that's linked. So let's pretend this is the third paragraph in the Forbes article below.

….. and that's why Paul Wall and Outkast will always make my list of the top rappers from the south. It's debated who to crown king or kings of the fast-spitting Midwest rappers, but for me, it's Bone Thugs…

Do you see above the title from the article I wrote on Now Entertainment was placed naturally within the middle of a paragraph on Forbes?

Anchor text is the word or words that are hyperlinked. It could be the words, "click here" at the end of a sentence or a random word within a sentence. If someone is writing about my website they may link back to my website by using the anchor text, "Now Entertainment" within a paragraph or even may use an artist's name that I referenced in an earlier article on my site as the anchor text.

Backlinks are like the online equivalent to being a local auto shop and being referred to as one of the best shops in town by multiple people. The more people singing your praises, the better, especially if those people are influential like the mayor (Forbes), the Sheriff (Washington Post), and the hottest chick in town (Vogue magazine).

(DA) Domain authority measures how likely a site is to rank on the first few pages within search results. If site (a) has a DA of 35 and site (b) has a DA of 65, and they both write a story about Eminem on the same day, site (b) is likely to show up on the first page of google search results and site (a) may also appear on the first page of results, but it will be further down the list of search engine results. If you have years of press coverage and all of the other sites have a higher DA, then site (a) may be found on page 5 or possibly 15.

How to get press

There are various ways to gain press coverage. Article placements on blogs, news, and magazines are commonly referred to as press, PR, or public relations. These services vary in their approach as some are traditional outreach, and some are paid placements.

The traditional method is where an agent typically sends you a basic questionnaire via email or contacts you by a phone call to learn more about you and your goals. They then create a brief well-written writeup about you accompanied by contact info and begin reaching out to their contacts at various online and print publications and pitch your story. Depending on your goals, they may reach out to local outlets only or worldwide. This can be very pricey, ranging anywhere from $300 to well over $5,000, and may ultimately yield few or no results at all. You have more of a chance in gaining strong press coverage this way when it involves a project featuring a huge celebrity or if there's an incredible and relevant backstory.

Agencies have already established relationships with many writers, and if you have a good story to pitch, they'll be able to land you a ton of press. A good agency will politely refuse to work with you if their values don't align with yours or if they feel you're not yet ready for the type of services they offer. Those in it strictly for the money will know ahead of time they're not going to be able to help you land anything and still take your money. So ask around before making your decision on which agency to sign a contract with.

Sometimes, depending on what you're seeking the press coverage for, it may be wise to plan your approach to reach out close to a relevant event or timeframe. For example, let's say you create an app centered around black empowerment; if you begin to reach out in January just before black history month, you will likely get a better response than reaching out during the Christmas holidays. Or, if you are a horrorcore rapper, Halloween may be your best bet when reaching out to gain placements.

In earlier days, I received a write-up on the local NBC News station. I was offered to speak on camera because of a campaign against suicide during the national suicide awareness week in September. We reached out to the news outlets in August, a month prior.

There are ways you can do this type of outreach yourself as well, but first, you need to be sure you have good grammar in your pitch and your approach is professional and respectful. I highly recommend using Grammarly to make sure your spelling and punctuation are on point. Secondly, please do not reach out saying, "yo, let's work," "Hey bro fuck with me" you get the point. A good email would be formatted similarly to the example below. I'm going to use italics to set the text apart in the model, but be clear you should not use italics.

Hey John, how are you? I hope you and yours are well!

I'm Stacy, founder of displaced gals of London. I recently read your article about Lucy's follow-up single to her debut hit, "love letter." I couldn't agree more with you, and you made some very valid points. The new video she co-produced truly showcases she's more than just a beautiful voice.

I'm a singer myself as well, and since we both share similar tastes in music, I thought I'd reach out to introduce myself and share my upcoming single with you. I'd love to know your thoughts and opinions on it.

(insert SoundCloud or YouTube link)

(insert link or attachment [preferably a link] to an EPK [electronic press kit] – a document with bio, social links, headshot, performance photo, music video, and any notable accomplishments such as awards & quotes from other significant writeups.

Thanks for your time, and have a great day!

Regards,

Stacy D. Lawson

Now in the above email, you've managed to introduce yourself, compliment them, and make your request. You don't want to go on and on; time is precious, curators and bloggers receive hundreds of proposals a day, and you don't want to waste their time. If they want to, they will review your EPK, but you can't force them. You shouldn't fill an email with unnecessary fluff, keep it direct and to the point, and please don't beg or tell them how you're the shit. Keep a friendly tone, pleasant and cordial. Never send Spotify links because they won't be able to listen to the song unless they have a paid Spotify account. And nobody likes download links; it fills up the computer's hard drive, can contain a virus, and most of all, the email may land in the spam folder per the automated spam filter.

Determining who to contact and how

Once you've decided what your pitch will be, it's time to find outlets that report on similar topics. If you're a hip-hop artist, you obviously won't contact outlets that report on rock bands or that don't write music-related content at all. The next thing you should do is read some of the articles on the website you intend to pitch and find staff writers and contributors who write about music and topics similar to yours.

A good bit of the time, writers stick to specific topics such as food, LGBTQ, politics, entertainment, business, fashion, etc., and do not stray from what they know best. At the top, bottom, or both top & bottom of articles, you'll find the author listed, and most of the time, if you click on their name, it will display their social media accounts, a brief bio, and maybe even their email. But if not then just type their name into a google search and you may be able to find their Muckrack or LinkedIn account.

So it's relatively easy to determine whom to reach out to, but how? Some authors will state how they prefer to be contacted in their bio. Others will list it in their Muck Rack or LinkedIn account if they have one. If they don't have their preference listed on either place, they will typically add a social link such as Twitter to their author bio, which may be where they prefer to be reached.

Another method to get ahold of them is to use a service such as Anymail Finder, SNOVio, Hunter, Contact out, or my personal favorite, Rocket Reach. These services will locate the target's email, socials, and sometimes even their phone numbers. But keep in mind you also have those who don't want to be reached and prefer only to write about topics they find themselves or are assigned to write about by their team. So tread carefully when using these services.

Pay to play

You can pay anyone to promote you, your business, or your product as long as it aligns with their audience and you have a decent budget. As far as social media goes, you can request a shoutout, story post, dance video, tutorial, review, or even make a video together, depending on your budget.

When it comes to paying for articles, you can reach out to blogs & magazines by email, as stated in the previous section. Still, this time instead of asking for a possible review, you can ask if they accept a guaranteed placement fee and what that cost might be. Most ethical journalists will frown upon this and will not respond, or they may politely decline. Never contact the editor with this type of request. To be completely honest, you might even want to create a secondary email address with a fake name and picture of an old white lady. It could increase your chances of receiving a response, wink wink.

If all else fails, you may still have an opportunity to get the placement by contacting the website using a generic form located on their contact page. You will see an option to "advertise with us" or a similar statement. Sometimes when you choose this option, a page will display all of their rates for various advertising types, whether that be a banner placement, article, or an entire front page twenty-four-hour takeover.

Many marketers have deals in place for placements that sometimes are a lot higher in cost or may very well be cheaper. For example, some sites offer one-off article placements for around $500, but buying in bulk may be $250 each. A marketer may buy ten slots upfront and then resale for $350 each and turn a profit that can be cheaper for you and lucrative for the marketer. But beware, some do the opposite and double or triple the prices and target novice artists and entrepreneurs, hyping them up about how it will make them superstars or generate a ton of sales, etc. Also, shop around if you choose to go this route because you may find something you initially perceive as exclusive and later find out Joe, Jimmy, and Jill all offer the same thing at different rates. Trust me, unfortunately I know personally, as I once paid $1,800 for something I later found as low as $400, ouch! Yes, in life and entrepreneurship especially, you will take similar hits; the point is to learn from your mistakes and move forward. Make sure to help others along your journey not make similar mistakes rather than preying on the naïve newcomer.

Press release distribution services.

There are many press release distribution services such as PR Newswire, Accesswire, EINnewswire, and more. These services take care of the leg work for you. You create the writeup and pay a fee anywhere from $100 - $700, and they distribute the content to various sites. The content will appear on the sites marked with tags such as "branded content, press release, originally seen on, sponsored" and other key indicators that it's a paid advertisement and not original reporting from a staff member of the sites where it appears. Sometimes it will state something like, "the views outlined in this article are not of our own, we did not take part in its creation nor endorse." Suppose you just want to get the word out about something quickly, such as your side of the story in an alleged crime. A board member stepping down, a member of your r&b group passing from a drug overdose, etc. in other words, something of significance that needs to be clarified asap. In that case, a press release is the quickest and most efficient route for you to take.

I've recently seen several social media businessmen and women taking advantage of young ignorant entrepreneurs by using these services and doubling the price tag. Now that you've read this, you'll begin to notice them as well. You'll start to see their paid ads or Instagram story posts saying, "swipe up now and get featured on Fox and other news sites within the next 24 hours."

I can't knock their hustle and would never call out names exposing their tactics publicly on social media. After all, we all have bills to pay, and that's precisely why you now have this information presented to you in the form of a book that you purchased, and I greatly appreciate it. And if you didn't pay for this book, well, my Cashapp is @OfficialNOWEnt make it happen; I've got bills too.

Why are you seeking press coverage in the first place?

A good question to ask yourself before wasting your time and money is why exactly you're seeking press coverage. Being able to answer this question will give you the ability to make smarter decisions. If you cannot answer this question, then nobody else can answer it for you. You surely do not want to throw money around, hoping for something to work but not even understand how or why it did or didn't.

Reasons, why one might seek press are to raise awareness about a product or service, attain a Wikipedia page or social media verifications, among other things. Whatever it is you're seeking will determine which outlets you target for your campaign.

Getting Verified

Everyone asks, "how'd you get verified? Can you help me get the badge, bro!?" Well, yes and no, let me explain. Many people ask about verification, and some feel they deserve it because they have a large following, but this is simply not true. I can't count the number of times I've been approached about getting the badge, especially from Tiktok creators with millions of followers. Upon explaining the prerequisites to them, they often get flustered and even angry with me like it's my fault they can't receive the badge.

All social media sites have different criteria for approval. Still, ultimately the badges are given to businesses and people with a clear need to be vetted as the correct brand or individual. For example, let's say you consider & categorize yourself as a model, and you've acquired a large Instagram following, but you've never been in a magazine or on a runway. You'd be considered an Instagram model, not a traditional model. And since your fame is only based on your Instagram following, there is no need to verify you. Now, suppose you also have written a book on marketing yourself as a model on Instagram, secured a deal with a large swimsuit brand, and have modeled their summer wear in a magazine or two. In that case, you deserve the verification because your notoriety comes from other places outside of the app itself.

I'll give you another example. Let's say you're a recording artist doing numbers on Tiktok. Still, the numbers don't match up with your Spotify listeners, and you haven't been spoken of on the news or blogs or toured, then you'd be considered a Tiktok rapper, and Tiktok verification isn't for you. On the other hand, if your Tiktok fame translates into similar Spotify monthly listeners. You've received press coverage for the last live show or podcast you were on, and you also have a large following on YouTube, then you'd be considered more than a Tiktok rapper and deserving of the badge on Tiktok.

The point is that you are known for other things outside of the platform where you're seeking the badge. This way, if a fan is looking you up on the said platform, they will find the right business or public figure to follow. It prevents the mass following of fake fan accounts or scammers posing as the real you.

Remember in the previous chapter when I mentioned that you should first know why you're seeking press as it will determine which outlets you target and how to go about your approach? Getting verified can be accomplished in different ways, but press coverage on key outlets is one. Before we dive into that, let's first focus on the easily attainable badges.

Currently, in 2020, if you release a song through CDbaby or Distrokid after its release, you can locate the claim official artist channel section in the settings tab of the distributor and verify your YouTube and Spotify accounts. I'm not going to give you the complete detailed walkthrough of how to verify the account, but it's an effortless task, and if you have any trouble, just contact your DSP. Things move at such a fast pace that some of this could no longer be relevant by the time you're reading it. For example, in early 2020, artists could verify their Cashapp accounts by linking them to their Spotify account. Although this is no longer a valid method to verify Cashapp accounts, it was a very lucrative time for those that held the secret of how to do it.

Another easily attainable verification is Google. Once your project is released, a Google knowledge panel should auto-generate and appear in Google search results for your artist name.

A knowledge panel is a rectangular box off to the right side of the google search results screen. It will include a picture, releases, social links, label name, and other information such as a Wikipedia bio snippet if you have one. If yours does not appear, try searching for your name again with the word "musician" beside it.

In small print, at the bottom of the panel, it will read, "claim this panel" click on it, and you'll be taken to the google verification form. You will be required to present a picture of yourself holding your government ID and a reason why you're claiming the panel. Simply state that you're claiming it to control your online presence. You'll also be asked to log into three or more social accounts and take a screenshot to upload. The reason for this is they can tell that you're logged in and not just a fan of the artist as the view of the social accounts dashboard will have elements that do not appear unless you're truly logged into the account, such as the "edit page" tab. This helps them make sure they're giving the correct individual access to the panel and not some random person out to ruin the reputation of an artist, entrepreneur, or entity.

The following two are not exactly easy, but they're not as hard to attain. The tab to request Audiomack and SoundCloud verifications are located in the settings section of the dashboard on these social sites, and the requirements aren't hard to meet at all. You have to be active and upload your music. Still, unlike other social platforms, it doesn't require press or have to do with anything other than being actively growing your following and getting plays, comments, & reposts. SoundCloud only seems to verify accounts with a following over 5k and a minimum of 30k or more plays on all of your songs.

To attain this, you will likely have to spend some money. Luckily for legit growth services, you can use the link in the bio of my company SoundCloud account or just type the following link into google manually repostexchange.com/hi?r=FJBDD and click enter. Stay away from the $50 for 1 million plays and followers fake fluff bots you find on google as SoundCloud can tell it's not real, plus you run the risk of being banned, primarily if your content is monetized. Other means to grow your account, such as using Repost Network by SoundCloud and applying to have your songs added to their playlists. Still, in my personal experience, it doesn't work well as they offer multiple playlists to submit to but limit your submissions to one song submission to only one of the playlists a month. If you have three songs, it will take you well over a year to submit to them all with this limitation.

When it comes to other social platforms, they're a bit more tricky. I'll try to break it down and simplify it as best I can. When a company creates a marketing app using Facebook & Instagram API (Application Programming Interface) and then spends a substantial amount of money using said app on ads, they can apply for a partnership with Facebook & Instagram. If accepted, they have a page open to them known as the partner portal and a direct employee contact at Facebook that will help them with various things. They typically want to keep the ad agency happy because the agency has a monthly ad spend of thousands of dollars and even higher.

Unlike the generic verification form presented to the public, the portal form allows for press links to be added to the verification submission for review, and rather than going through a robot review to pass particular prerequisites prior to being passed along to a human; the portal request goes directly to the assigned partner. If there are any issues with the application, the Facebook employee can let the agency know so that the application can be fixed and approved. In comparison, the generic form does not give information on your denial. For example, you may meet all verification requirements, but you might have your page categorized under the wrong category. Unless you fix this, you'll never be approved nor know why you continue to be denied. With that said, connecting with someone that has partner portal access is your best bet or approval. These types of submissions are often offered on the black market for anywhere from $1500 - $10,000. You might ask, why so much? The reasoning behind this is that those with portal access #1 can lose access to the portal and even their partnerships with the social company because the ability to submit via the portal is to be reserved as a free service to show appreciation to the ad client. Reason two is that spaces are limited. Suppose the agency sells this service to you for, let's say, $500. A potential ad client comes along and is interested in signing a fifteen thousand plus ad contract with the agency but wants their account verified upfront. In that case, the agency will not be able to provide it and thus may lose the potential client to another ad agency that has open slots. If you find someone claiming to sell verification via partner portal for a few hundred bucks, it's highly likely to be a scam.

If you're lucky like I was, you can have your verifications taken care of by way of bartering. For example, my personal Facebook profile was taken care of by an agency that did not have a google knowledge panel for their business. I knew how to create one for them, and rather than paying someone $600-$900 to make them one, we made a simple trade.

Often, for musicians, a good distribution company will already have partnerships in place with these social platforms and can submit on your behalf. Although most won't offer it, and unless you're already doing good streaming numbers and you request them to do so, you may never even know they possess the ability to submit via the portal.

The thing about businesses that involve tech is that they're continually evolving and what works today may not work tomorrow. For this reason, you must stay in a constant state of learning and networking, or the information you have will become outdated, and you'll be out of the loop. With that said, at this moment, in 2020, Facebook requires you to have ten or more articles submitted along with your verification request for approval, and Instagram requires fifteen or more. Also, if requesting the badge for a business, you will need a trademark to go along with the application as well.

The press coverage cannot be on any run-of-the-mill website either. Reputable news sites and magazines must cover it. But be careful about the coverage you attain when it comes to this process. You can be easily duped by smooth-talking marketers when it comes to this type of stuff if you don't know your shit. Please refer to the previous chapter on how to get press for more info.

WATCH YOUR ASS

In this chapter, we'll discuss a few things to watch out for as this game is full of snakes looking to make a buck off the backs of the hardworking unenlightened musicians and noobpreneurs. I've experienced my fair share of mistakes that cost me dearly, and I would hate for others working towards bringing their dreams into reality to make the same mistakes. There is no sure-fire way to guarantee that you will not face failure at times; the key is never to accept defeat!

There's nothing wrong with shopping around before making business decisions. Anyone who makes it a point to have you believe their product or service is rare, or there's a scarcity most likely is attempting to play on your emotions and make you feel like you have to make a purchase right away. Some sites even go to the extent of adding fake countdown clocks or automated posts that pop up saying Joe from Iowa just purchased x amount, then two seconds later boom Jill from Florida bought...etc. You get the point.

You have to use your judgment when it comes to certain situations. I find it best to trust my gut feeling. The majority of the time, when I don't, it blows up in my face. As I previously mentioned, things shift all the time in this industry because a lot of it has to do with tech and policies, so sometimes there may very well be a situation where time is of the essence. For example, there was a point in time where YouTube did not require 100k subscribers for verification. Similarly, before Twitter made their verification form public, anyone that had $50 to spend on Twitter ads could access a hidden verification form. I learned about this when I stumbled upon the form and sent the link to an artist friend of mine by the name of Shotgun Shane. When he opened the link, it took him to a generic FAQ page about verification, but on my end, the same link presented me with an actual application form. We went over everything to see if there were any differences in our accounts at the time and what it all boiled down to was that I had previously run a few ads, and he had not.

Business is booming in the black market for stolen accounts. One of the worst things that can happen to an artist is to have their social accounts hijacked. The hacker can be hateful and make a complete mockery of you, or they can delete everything you've ever posted and then sell the account to someone else on the black market for a decent amount. I've seen many accounts for sale in various niches at prices ranging anywhere from $500 - $20,000 depending on how large a following and the demographic.

Hackers are becoming savvier when it comes to this operation. I've received DM's from real-life friends saying things like. "yo bro look at this picture of you wtf" with a link below the message to an Instagram post. When I clicked the link, it brought me to a copycat site and asked me to log in. If you don't notice the URL is a bit different or a section of Instagram isn't clickable etc., and login, you just handed over your password to a hacker. What happened in my situation was someone found a hole in the code of an app that my friend had granted Facebook login access. He and thousands of others playing the seemingly innocent virtual card game were all having DM's sent out from their accounts by the hacker without them even knowing. This is why Facebook and other socials display a message that says to make sure you trust the third-party app you're giving access to your account.

Make sure you add two-step verification within the settings section of all of your accounts and, if possible, add additional security such as a Yubikey. Adding a 2-step validation is done by adding a phone number or using apps such as Google authenticator to receive an additional login code for each login attempt. A Yubikey is a small device that looks similar to a USB drive that is the third line of defense against hackers. Make for damn sure if you switch phone numbers, you disable this setting before and reenable after you receive your new number, or you may lock yourself out of your account.

Watch out for people pretending to be a part of companies that ask for you to create a business Facebook account and give them access to your ads account! They will offer you thousands of dollars to run ads on your page, but in reality, they're just tricking you into signing over your account to them. I experienced this with an artist as well. The crazy part about it was that he asked me about it first, and after I did a bit of investigating I told him it would be a mistake to take any part of it. Yet, because of the lure of easy money, he took the chance anyway and lost his account.

First of all, the email had a few misspellings indicating it was likely fake as true professionals use programs like Grammarly to correct spelling, punctuation and check for plagiarism. They're also likely to proofread their content before sending it. The leading indicator was that they wanted him to give them access to his ads account. That would only be necessary if he had hired an ads agency to run ads for his content as they would need access to his account and billing information, etc. Had he taken the free Facebook blueprint classes, he would have known this and that anyone looking to target his audience could do so without having access to his account.

The business is notorious for fake friends looking to use you to benefit themselves until you're no longer of any value to them and then cut you lose. Some even throw dirt on your name afterward. If you're a kind-hearted person and lack discernment, some assholes in this business can and will break your spirit. But don't let it get you discouraged or cause you to repeat the process on others. Instead, take it as a lesson learned and move forward. Now and again, you will find those that aren't in the business of screwing people over. Making a few good connections like these and nurturing the relationships will ultimately lead you down the path to more positive associations. Before you know it, you will have developed a strong network of responsible, hardworking, and trustworthy individuals. You'll then begin to really feel the statement you've heard many say before, "your network is your net worth."

KNOW YOUR AUDIENCE

Know your audience. What does that even mean? It's a term you will find loosely used in every industry worldwide, but what does it mean? It means more than just researching the demographics or psychographics of your market. It also requires you to know yourself fully and what you are selling at any given moment. You need to be on point with what you want in this industry before you can even begin to expect someone else to buy into what you are selling, figuratively and literally. When an entrepreneur truly knows their audience, they're prepared to speak on it at any point, with anyone they come across.

Once you have defined your brand and place in the market, knowing your audience pretty much just means knowing how to deliver your message to certain people. If you are speaking with a professional, you want to be professional and not use slang. You want to have a variety of ways to deliver your message—practice code-switching. Code-switching is a way to communicate and depends on who you're speaking with but involves various hand gestures, facial expressions, and word choices. Using the same tone, vocabulary, slang, and mannerisms of whom you are communicating with will place you on common ground and seemingly make them feel more comfortable around you.

For example, my wife is a teacher. When she is speaking with her boss, she maintains eye-contact, keeps her hands still, uses the professional vocabulary of her field, and does a lot of head nodding and says, "yes mam." When a cop pulls her over, she is doe-eyed, suddenly has a southern accent, name drops that she is a teacher, and is overly respectful with a huge smile. Get a mirror and deliver your message in many ways switching up your mannerism. This way, no matter who you are speaking with, you will be appealing to them. Not knowing your audience can definitely cost you in this business. If your vocabulary is not up to par, how will you speak to CEOs when you have finally worked your way up to that level? Speaking to a CEO the same way to talk to your homeboys will not get you the deal you are looking to attain. For example, I once contacted a Twitter employee, and when asked how I was able to locate this particular representative, my dumbass said I used such and such tool to find my mark. Yikes, yes I don't know what in the total fuck I was thinking when I called her my mark but needless to say I never heard from her again.

Knowing your audience isn't easy; you have to put in the work. It takes a lot of research, and remember, in this industry, you are Never Off Work.

The Bottom Line

We all love music, and honestly, the majority of people have, at one point or another in their life, wished they could be a Rockstar. Unfortunately, it's just not meant to be for everyone. Many have unique talents such as graphic design and video animation, business, and producing or engineering. Some can write hit songs but can't sing. Some are charming and can network and sell anything. But it seems nowadays everyone wants to be a rapper. You have to realize that there are a ton of people who can rap. I've even seen soccer moms that can freestyle. For clarification, when I say freestyle, I don't mean rapping something live that was prewritten. That's not a freestyle! I'm referring to coming up with a rap on the spot. If I can't point to an object and you begin rapping about it, then you can't freestyle!

Enough with my rant. Everyone on the team wants to be a rapper these days, and it's why many fail at their pursuit to the top. If a conversation took place with the homies about what everyone in the crew's strengths was and who needed to take care of what, there would be more success stories. You likely have a friend that's good with a camera and graphic design, but he wants to be a rapper. You probably have another friend that can play the piano because his grandmother taught him in church, but rather than learning how to produce, he also wants to be a rapper. Then, of course, you have a buddy that is a wiz when it comes to tech stuff and could build your website and run your social media, but he also wants to be a damn rapper. Finally, you have the one guy out of your crew that is the best at rapping and should lead the way. But guess what he has no real support from the guys around him that could all work together to make all their dreams come true. Nobody wants to take the backseat and invest their time and money into one person. If they did, they could jump on the mic later after generating some money and success. That's a big part of the problem because to make it you need a team. There have to be those in the front and those in the background. So if you cannot develop a real team you must be ready to learn and work your ass off. Taking care of all of the necessary work until you can form a solid team later down the road.

If you can get your team on the same page, you must figure out how you will finance your career. If you want to make music and do local shows, and that's all, then you're good to go, but if you're going to go mainstream, it's time to realize that talent alone isn't going to get you there. It costs money to make it in this game and if you have no intentions of investing in yourself, then make sure you're attending college or looking for a good job because you're not going to make it boss.

If you're not working towards building your dream daily, it's not happening. If you don't have trouble falling asleep because a new drum pattern pops in your head or you keep turning on the light to write down a new line that just came to you as you were about to drift off, and if you're not waking and making micro goals and reaching at least one or two of them every day then forget it. You have to really live this shit; it has to consume you! If not, then before you know it, years will have passed, and you'll still be in the same spot, still dreaming and talking about what your plans are instead of having achieved some of them by that point. And if you're not those guys, then get ready for the backlash because once you've made moves and brought some of your dreams into fruition, those other guys will begin to hate you and say you've changed. They'll throw dirt on your name simply because they can't take responsibility for their own actions. They can't look at themselves in the mirror and realize they themselves are why they made no progress. They procrastinated, didn't make the sacrifices, and wasted precious time fucking off; now they have to blame somebody else, and you become the target.

What I've noticed holding most people back is that they don't recognize what they're truly gifted at and double down on it. You have to stay true to self. Maybe even ask others outside of your close family and friends their opinions on your personality and what your good at.

ABOUT THE AUTHOR

Tony started his career path as a rapper in the 7th grade when a friend Rico passed him a song he had written. Tony wrote a piece in response to Rico's, and this back and forth continued for the next few years. Tony was living with his grandmother at the time because his dad was busy running the streets. His mother had to work long hours, so she wasn't around much. When his dad was around, there was always a lot of fighting; you know, the typical abusive stuff.

Tony's parents had been divorced for years but continued living together for his sake, although it would have honestly been best if they were in separate households. When his dad was around, his mother slept on the couch, stayed in the bathroom reading the bible, and played video games in Tony's room while he slept; pretty much anything to avoid his father's drunken rage. She developed some health issues that caused her to gain a lot of weight and lose her hair, but the doctors couldn't determine what caused it.

At this point, his father's physical abuse turned into mental abuse, making fun of her, etc.

This was what led to Tony living with his grandmother; he just couldn't take it anymore.

Over the years, his father's anger grew worse. Finally, his mother got up the courage to move out for good but into a bad neighborhood as it was all she could afford at the time while working in a carpet factory. Tony began lashing out at school seemingly for no good reason, although now, as an adult, he now understands it was just his anger and frustration coming out in the wrong ways.

Tony's grandmother fell ill and had to move in with his dad, so Tony went along as well. Shortly afterward, she passed, and Tony was cleared to stay home from school the day after her funeral but made a choice to go because he needed someone to talk to about how he was feeling. He went to his first class with his girlfriend, and afterward, on the way to the gym to take their break, he felt the urge to leave, so he pulled her aside and was in the middle of telling her bye when he thought he heard someone call his name. He looked around, but the hallway was full of students and staff, and he didn't notice anyone waving or any sign that someone had actually called his name. He passed it off as either he heard wrong, or somebody had called someone else with the same name, but this wasn't the case. A teacher had apparently called his name. She was trying to get his attention to get me back in line to the gym, and when he looked up, he had also looked in her direction, and although he didn't see her, she thought he did and was ignoring her, so she decided to come up and snatch him by the arm to pull him into the office.

When he felt the jerk of his arm, his immediate reaction was to snatch his arm back before turning to look. He didn't know what was happening, but she had pulled him with such force in one direction that when he snatched his arm back, it resulted in the teacher falling to the ground like in a game of tug-of-war when one side lets loose of the rope. She was embarrassed and told the principal he had pushed her down, which resulted in him being arrested. While in the office waiting to go to jail, he overheard her say to the janitor, "you have to speak up for me," and he laughed and replied, "I wasn't there. I was down by the middle school. Besides, he might come after me then."

On the day of court, Tony had six witnesses testify that he didn't shove her at all. One of the students had just started school that day and had no reason to lie for him; they had never even met. The judge asked if she went to the doctor because of the back pain claims, and the answer she gave was, but of course, no. Coincidently the school cameras were in a blind spot and didn't catch any of it. It seemed that Tony would be set free, but then the janitor, her only witness, said Tony did push her, and it sealed his fate. The prosecution was seeking six years but luckily he received only five months of incarceration and a year of probation afterward.

When he was released, by chance, he started dating her niece. He learned that the teacher had mental issues and was on various medications for it. None of her family had anything to do with her. She had been cheating on her husband with the schoolhouse's janitor, the same one that spoke on her behalf in court. All because of her pride, she couldn't let it go. Tony now knew she had him locked up because she was embarrassed and someone needed to pay. Of course, it couldn't have been that she made a mistake! Tony also later learned the judge owned part of the private facility that he sent him to do his time, which meant that Tony filling the bed put dollars in the judge's pocket.

Tony was bitter but later realized it was God's intervention because he was headed down the wrong path for sure. It may have very well prevented him from actually doing something that may have caused him to be locked up a lot longer or even possibly dead. Because prior to this, he was constantly in fights, drugs, alcohol, etc., you name it.

His dad was in the middle of a court battle with his aunts over his grandmother's money. Tony asked not to be dragged into it, but he was, and when the judge ruled against his father because of something Tony said in court, his father kicked him out and wouldn't let him take any of his stuff not even his clothes.

Tony moved in with his mom and joined the local church. He began running the soundboard as well as took a spot in the choir. This further fueled his interest in music, and he started writing again. Tony found that writing was a great way to release his inner demons rather than lashing out. "I can say for sure that music saved me from God only knows what", he once said.

Tony started work at a local car dealership cutting the grass and washing cars. He walked to work and created a savings account that he later used to buy himself a bed and new clothes. One day on his walk to work, it started raining, and his dad drove by, flipped him off, and hollered fuck you. He had made it clear he wasn't interested in a relationship ever again.

As time went on, Tony saved up for a used car, and started going to talent shows and even landed an offer for a recording contract with a local label. But he had recently had a child, and life on the road wasn't going to be a great idea at that time in his life, so he passed up the offer.

After a failed marriage Tony was left to raise his six and seven-year-old girl and boy, with by himself as a single dad.

But not long before that occurred, his ex-wife's cousin was living with them. He was going through a divorce himself and killed himself with a gun that Tony handed him on Halloween night. Tony felt responsible for it for a long time, so he ran a campaign against suicide, mentioned on NBC news in later years. https://41nbc.com/2018/09/20/292361/

Tony raised his kids at that point by himself, making just two dollars over the allowed limit to receive government assistance. His kid's mother didn't pay child support either or hardly ever come around, and it's still that way today. They struggled to live in a trailer with leaks in the roof and holes in the floor. They had no heat, so they heated the home with the stove, etc. Tony looked in the mirror one day and knew he needed to do something, or this was going to be their life forever because he had no wiggle room to get them into any better situation. So he started going to school for the music business and became a truck driver, which made more money than his previous job as a forklift driver. He drove 2 hours to and from work, leaving him with hardly any time for sleep. He took the extra money he had and invested in recording & video equipment, and got them a house in the suburbs. He ended up quitting school because it would of ended up costing him too much, but he took what he learned and began to build Now Entertainment.

Tony started by recording & releasing material from local acts with the intent to create a record label. Where Tony is from, there are not many jobs and a lot of poverty. It wasn't about the money; he genuinely wanted to help change their lives. After all, he recognized the downward spiral they were on because he was once traveling the same road. But after some time, it was clear to see they weren't as serious about it as he was. They didn't really believe or have it in them to make the necessary moves to progress; it was more of a hobby or playing the lottery to them. He had wasted a good bit of money investing into their careers, but luckily he also learned how to do graphic work, website coding, production, video editing, and more while working with them.

While working with them, he also had the idea to start a blog section on their website and write about other artists. The concept behind it was to draw free traffic to their site via the artists he wrote about sharing the content to their friends, fans, and family. This would then lead them to our music and merch and translate into being fans of our content and customers he thought.

Later, after giving free advice to many artists, managers, and even other well-established magazine owners like Just Jay of Hype Magazine, he thought to himself, I can really help other artists with this by shining light onto their art. I can learn from them and grow myself and also offer label services versus running a label, especially when the traditional label structures were falling apart. More and more artists were looking to be independent.

Right after he helped DJ Khaled's former artist Nino Brown attain a sweet distribution deal and verify his Instagram account, he had a conversation where Nino asked him to be his full-time manager over coach K the biggest manager in the game at the time. It was flattering, but Tony didn't feel he was ready at the time and would hinder his career, so he didn't take him up on the offer, but it gave him the drive and determination he needed to legalized Now Entertainment Magazine and push forward.

Shortly afterward, a friend and family member of one of the local musicians he started with passed away in jail after being refused water and beaten by guards. http://hiphopweekly.com/now-entertainment-establishes-website-to-highlight-social-issues-police-brutality/

https://www.thehypemagazine.com/2019/02/now-entertainment-is-gearing-up-to-drop-album-dedicated-to-antonio-may/

Tony connected with Christian Vind, and they became good friends. Tony loved Christian's energy and began to teach him what he'd learned, and Vind began to write for his magazine. They realized they held the same values and had similar goals, so they planned to form a partnership

https://respect-mag.com/2019/11/now-entertainment-introduces-new-app/

Tony began writing and reaching out to top celebrities. At the same time, I continued building in other respects, such as the iOS app and finding financing for our amazon channel and interview equipment. But not long after, Vind had somewhat of a mental block and had to take a step back and focus on his family.

Tony started writing tip-based articles on Forbes & Entrepreneur. But he soon realized he wasn't going to be allowed to say all that he thought needed to be told via their platform, so he decided to put it in a book.

He recently recorded a song with Xpression the MC and Layzie Bone of the legendary rap group Bone Thugs -N- Harmony. The group heavily influenced Tony as a teenager, and this was like the icing on the cake as things come full circle.

"I've been able to work with many different nationalities and learn about various cultures. Interviewed former diplomates and helped grow artist's careers from their first video shoot to buying their first home from the money they made with their music. I wouldn't change a thing about the path I chose, those I've met, and what I've learned along the way. It's indeed been a blessing." --- Tony

After raising his kids from ages 6 & 7 until they were 11 & 12, he got remarried, ironically to a school teacher, and had another daughter during the beginning of the pandemic; a bit scary, to say the least. She's now eleven months old, and they're expecting another child in August 2021.

www.ingramcontent.com/pod-product-compliance
Lightning Source LLC
LaVergne TN
LVHW021740060526
838200LV00052B/3376